1984, an ill-advised journey?

Colette and David Nicolle

Copyright © 2021 Colette and David Nicolle

ISBN: 9798473180152

All rights reserved, including the right to reproduce this book, or portions thereof in any form. No part of this text may be reproduced, transmitted, downloaded, decompiled, reverse engineered, or stored, in any form or introduced into any information storage and retrieval system, in any form or by any means, whether electronic or mechanical without the express written permission of the author.

Introduction

David and Colette Nicolle spent four years living in Jordan where David was teaching Art History at Yarmouk University, in what was then the small northern town of Irbid. These were also the only four years in their married life when Colette was not working full-time and during which David was the family's main wage-earner. Yet they were hardly a rest-cure for Colette. David had gone to Jordan in the late summer of 1983, to see whether the job was real and whether Colette should follow him. This left Colette literally holding the baby, namely young Freddie who was then a little over one-year old, as well as holding down a teaching job at Hendon College of Further Education - in a building now used by Middlesex University - in north London. David's job proved to be real, as was Yarmouk University and the accommodation which the University offered to its married staff. So Colette and Freddie flew to Amman shortly before Christmas 1983.

This book recounts the journey which the Nicolle family undertook during the summer of 1984. Ever since, David and Colette had dreamed of producing this account of their notes, diaries and photos, but it was only when they reached retirement that they had the time to do so.

Antoinette (for many years later known as Nette) is included in this story, but unaware of the goings-on as she was then in utero. The trip was undertaken partially out of a sense of adventure, partly because David, having driven the route several times before, wanted to share the experience with Colette, and partly because David wanted to visit a number of culturally significant sites to take photographs and undertake some research. The most important of these were to have been the painted late-medieval monasteries of northern Romania - which, in the event, the travellers never reached.

Looking north-west across the campus of Yarmouk University late in 1983.
The clear winter air means that the distant hills of the Israeli-occupied Golan Heights
in southern Syria can be seen in the far distance.

However, there was a background which might explain why David felt so confident that he, accompanied by a somewhat less confident Colette and a blissfully unaware Freddie, could undertake such a trip in complete expectation of no problems. David had, in fact, been travelling to and through much of the Middle East since the mid-1960s, having already driven overland to the Balkans, Turkey, Syria, Lebanon, Jordan, Iraq and Iran on several occasions. Colette's experience was more limited, but she had back-packed to these countries, with the exception of Lebanon and Iran, with her new husband David back in 1978.

1978 - Colette's first experience of the Middle East

David and Colette had been married just over two years and still believed that anything was possible. To be frank, they still do! In 1978 David kept a diary of their travels, leaving Edinburgh (where he was studying for his PhD) on 30th June and finally arriving back in London on 11th August, while Colette sent regular postcards to her father-in-law, Patrick (Pat) Nicolle, in Mill Hill, London. Two quotations might shed light on their tendency to naive optimism. The first is from a postcard written by Colette around July 13th:

> Dear Pat,
>
> After a very long train journey (train hit truck, later reported derailment and/or broken track & misconnection) having a lovely time in Istanbul. Different from everything I've ever known, chaotic & cheap, & such interesting food. David has been working very hard, of course, at the Topkapi museum, but I've spent my time with a couple from Aberdeen. Safety in numbers! Then we met David late afternoon. We're spending 4 nights here, so it gives us enough time to rest up before the trip right across Turkey to the Syrian border. I do <u>love</u> it here, much to David's delight.
>
> Love, Colette

The following is David's diary entry for Monday, 31st July, when the couple started the homeward leg of their journey, setting off from the Jordanian capital of Amman across northern Jordan where, five years later, they would begin what was probably the most extraordinary period of their married life:

No breakfast except a glass of tea, before getting our service-taxi for Damascus. It went round the houses a bit, collecting other fares, including a stop at a convent for an itinerant nun, where we got a cup of coffee as well. The drive to Damascus was easy, through pleasant scenery, hills in northern Jordan (*actually passing within a few kilometres of the town of Irbid with the new Yarmouk University campus, and alongside a vast fenced area where Yarmouk University hoped to build a much larger campus in the future - but never did*), lava strewn plains dotted with SAM (*Surface-to-Air anti-aircraft defence missile*) sites in southern Syria. The frontier was a piece of cake, the easiest in the Middle East so far. The taxi station wasn't far from the Funduq Arabi (*a little hotel in Damascus*) where John, Cynthia and I stayed back in '74 (*during the latter part of a trip during which the three drove a Mini to Iran and back*). In fact I found it much more easily than expected. Once settled in - very cheaply - we went off to check on transport to Istanbul. After a great deal of hassle we found that a bus did go direct from Damascus, unfortunately not on days useful to us. So we booked a bus to Aleppo in the hope of getting things arranged from there. During all this wandering about, we found the Suq (*bazaar*) - almost unintentionally - and even the "Stephan" shop, totally unintentionally (*one of the best and most reliable shops in the famous Suq Hamidiya, where Colette would later become a loyal customer*). In there, while looking at fine silk scarves, we saw Caroline Tantum (*whose husband worked in the British Embassy in Amman*) with some friends! They were buying large sheets of silk for gowns. We were quibbling about a small scarf that in the end we didn't buy. After a bit of a lie-down (*at the hotel*), since I had caught a touch of heat exhaustion, we toddled off to the National Museum. None of the Directorate staff were around, so I couldn't get permission to photograph. Instead I noted down everything to be dealt with tomorrow, when the Museum is closed to the public and hence more available to specialist student-work. By the end of this I was practically spark-out, so we had a quick tea in the nicest tea-garden in Damascus - all fountains and trees and a bill for well over one pound! Colette was hungry, and we agreed that I should eat something, so we went to the Etoile Restaurant, again of 1974 vintage (*just outside Bab Tuma in the Christian eastern quarter of the city*) where we had had lunch. I groped around a meat stew and some lovely sweet, sticky rice pudding. Back at the hotel I lay on my back and burned for an hour, before sleeping the sleep of the exhausted and the just.

The first year in Jordan, from 1983 to 1984

The months from the beginning of the academic year in autumn 1983 until the overland journey home during the summer of the following year were also eventful, in their own right. During the first term teaching at Yarmouk University David (known as "Dr. David") got to know his students and established a pattern of student trips to archaeological and cultural sites in various parts of Jordan. He was already living the eventful life of a somewhat underpaid British ex-pat in one of the Middle East's less wealthy countries.

Perhaps the best thing about doing Dr. David's Islamic Art and Architecture course was the field trips. Ruined Umayyad "desert palaces" like this one at Mshatta might be interesting, but getting away from the University in the company of other young people of the opposite sex was best of all. David is standing at the back with his hair blown up into a "Tintin quiff".

Having convinced Colette that the job at Yarmouk University really did exist, and that life could be fun, David was delighted when his wife and infant son Freddie arrived. Not taking any chances and always extra cautious, she had sought and been granted a leave of absence from Hendon College of Further Education, just in case it all turned out to be a horrible mistake.

Colette and Freddie, newly arrived in Jordan, with our faithful Fiat Panda and its Jordanian temporary number plate, outside our block of flats in Southern Housing in Yarmouk University campus.

He then set about demonstrating the values of the "new man", while Colette did the same with the values of the "liberated woman".

David and Freddie in his stroller demonstrating how a Western "new man" looks after his children, walking down the "main street" of Yarmouk University campus.

Freddie's early enthusiasm for Roman columns, here demonstrated at Umm Qays or the Gadara of ancient times, caused widespread amusement and a firm conviction that this was somehow an infant of considerable intelligence - not far wrong either!

Planned or otherwise, Colette also became pregnant, almost certainly at Karak during a familiarization tour around southern Jordan in January 1984. She had only been in the country for a few weeks and her loving husband David was, of course, very pleased to see her. Colette's new condition would have a certain bearing on the course of the drive back to England later that year.

Our first Fiat Panda making a detour to Mount Nebo while on the way to Karak in southern Jordan, with a locally made infant's cot tied to the roof-rack.

Colette on the veranda of the Government Rest-House at Karak, looking towards the Dead Sea and Palestine beyond. She was about twelve hours pregnant with Antoinette, though neither of us realized it at the time.

Karak Castle with the town and its Government Rest House on the right.

For Freddie, of course, the visit to southern Jordan was an exciting opportunity to meet other children of his own age, some of whom lived in tents and were quite at ease with huge animals called camels. By 1984 David and Colette were, or thought they were, seasoned Middle Eastern travellers while Freddie accepted anything this strange wide world had to offer.

Freddie getting to know some of the local children at the Bedouin encampment in Wadi Rum in the early spring of 1984.

And so here begins the trip from Irbid, Jordan, to London in June 1984, told through the separate, and at that time private, diaries of David and Colette.

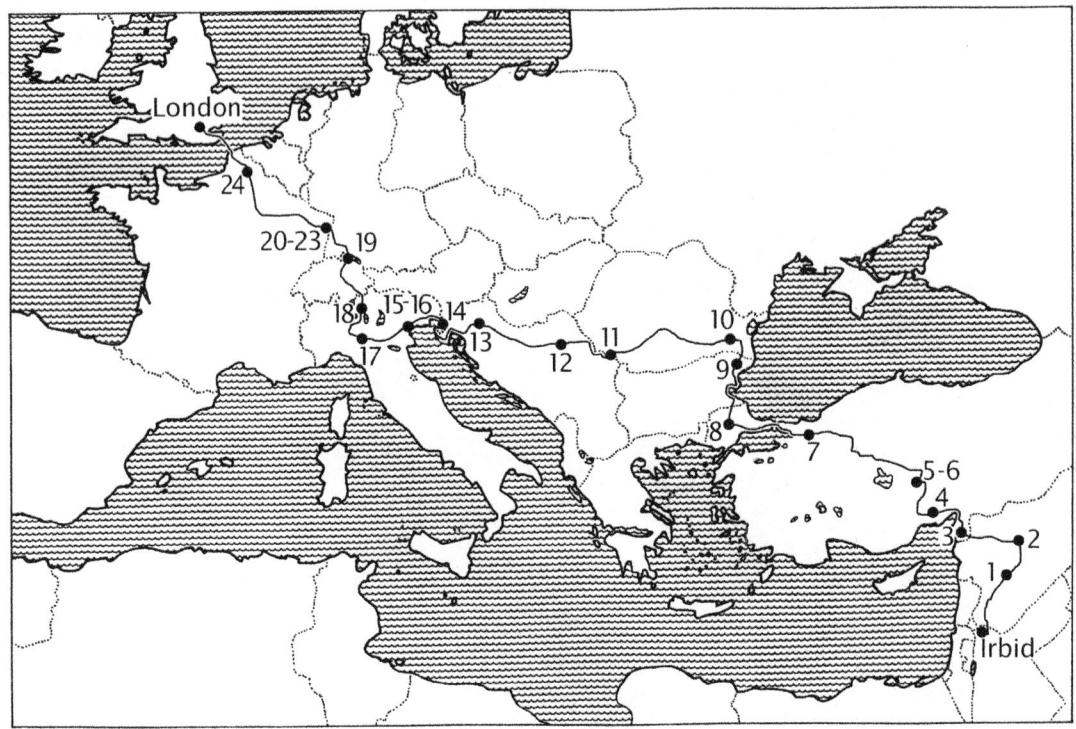

(Frontiers as existed in 1984; Route and night stops numbered)

Map Key

1 – Palmyra, Syria (15th June)

2 – Raqqa, Syria (16th June)

3 – Reyhanlı, Turkey (17th June)

4 – Adana, Turkey (18th June)

5 & 6 – Ürgüp, Turkey (19th & 20th June)

7 – Bolu, Turkey (21st June)

8 – Lüleburgaz, Turkey (22nd June)

9 - Tolbuhin [now Dobrich], Bulgaria (23rd June)

10 – Călărași, Romania (24th June)

11 - Donji Milanovac, Yugoslavia [now Serbia] (25th June)

12 – Belgrade, Yugoslavia [now Serbia] (26th June)

13 – Vrbovsko, Yugoslavia [now Croatia] (27th June)

14 – Trieste, Italy (28th June)

15 & 16 – Venice, Italy (29th & 30th June)

17 – Parma, Italy (1st July)

18 - Fino Mornasco [Como], Italy (2nd July)

19 – Constance, Italy (3rd July)

20 to 23 – Ittenheim, near Strasbourg, France (4th to 7th July)

24 – Arras, France (8th July)

Driving from Irbid, Jordan to London, England, June 1984

Friday, 15th June – Map: 1 Palmyra, Syria

David's Version

Away by 9 - which was amazing, considering pregnant wife and baby. Didn't get far though. I should have had a letter from the University to allow me out of the country. Bloody cheek! I kicked up a fuss and mentioned Major Abed, Cliff's pal (*Cliff was one of David's American colleagues, who was also a friend of one of the senior officers at the Jordanian frontier post*) but this didn't make any difference. Was driving back to the University to get a letter from Major Ghanmah (*the senior police officer in Irbid town*) when Major Abed overtook us, flagged us down and escorted us back to the frontier. He helped us through all the hassle, even the car papers. This done, we headed for the tough one - the Syrian frontier. Even this wasn't as bad as last time, though bad enough. Perhaps a Ramadan Friday made everything easier, certainly quieter. Got slightly ripped off by two youngsters who helped us through the paper maze, but even they had earned at least part of their tips. Glad to be clear, however. Freddie behaved himself very well almost to Palmyra. Had a bit of trouble finding the Duma and Dumayr road, but once on this then everything was straightforward. Dumayr airbase was full of stuff, with fighters lined up on the tarmac and a huge Soviet freighter coming in to land. Sun had set by time we reached Palmyra, behind some steep hills. The desert hereabouts is much more scenic than in Jordan. Freddie was unhappy by now, and screaming. Almost got desperate enough to go into the new - and very posh - Meridian Hotel. This would have cost 280 Syrian pounds. Instead ended up at the old, traditional Zenobia Hotel next to the main ruins of Palmyra,[1] for 69 Syrian pounds. All cleaned up, went for kofta supper next door. Now considering buying a sort of bolster made of carpeting as a local souvenir. Incidentally, one petrol can and the oil can were leaking all over the roof, so had to ditch these and reorganise the roof-rack. In the end we bought the carpet bolster thing for 135 Syrian. It's made here in Palmyra, on one of those narrow looms laid on the ground. Must remember to fill up with petrol tomorrow. I went for a short walk into town before turning in. Very windy but no mosquitoes. A good night's sleep.

Colette's Version

(*5 months pregnant*)

Got up at 6.30 and thought we did quite well to leave before 9.00.

Syrian frontier wouldn't let us pass until David got a letter from Badran (*from Yarmouk University*). Blew his top. Phoned Yarmouk. Left to get letter, but we were chased by Major Abed who fixed things for us.

Drove across desert on good road to Palmyra.

Too late to stop really (7.30 pm). Poor Freddie - he was tired and hungry. It's 8.30 by Syrian time, although we're going to stay on Jordanian time since it changes back again in Turkey.

Observations

Two Thermos flasks - one for milk and one for juice. We must have been dehydrated as I had headache by end of day. Plenty of food in car (bananas, biscuits, rolls from my Norwegian friend Lisa) and two bottles of water. Difficult to pee in desert with no trees. Found a small rubbish tip to hide behind. Need extra bottle of water for washing hands. Sponge on floor for Freddie's bed.

Colette, whose experience of marriage already included perhaps too much archaeology, and Freddie who was still new to the experience, in the Roman theatre at Palmyra. It was being restored at the time but, this being the Middle East, pregnant women and little children were quite free to wander around.

Palmyra with its classical ruins, set in the heart of the Syrian desert, is one of the most extraordinary places in the world. To appreciate it fully, however, the visitor needs to suffer just a little to get there. In our case that meant a long drive in a Fiat Panda - of course without air conditioning - on the direct desert road from Damascus.

The drive from Palmyra to the Euphrates Valley followed a road which simply did not exist when David first made this trip many years earlier. Yet the route across the desert is still marked by the bones of camels that did not make it back in the days when this was one of the toughest caravan routes in the Middle East.

The octagonal minaret of Meskene[2] is a remarkable and dramatic structure, standing alone on the edge of the escarpment overlooking man-made Lake Assad. The decorative bands and inscriptions are of brickwork, reflecting an architectural style that goes back to the very dawn of human history in the Euphrates Valley.

In the 1970s the early 13th century minaret of Meskene had to be moved brick by brick before the ruins of the abandoned medieval town disappeared as the water of Lake Assad rose behind the newly constructed Euphrates Dam near Raqqa.

Freddie was the patient hero of this journey, hot, sweating, dusty and all too often sitting in a damp nappy. Colette was pretty heroic as well and while her monomaniac husband shot off the road to visit an obscure piece of medieval Islamic architecture - in this case at Meskene in north-eastern Syria - she did what mothers do.

Saturday 16th June – Map: 2 Raqqa, Syria

David's version

A hard but successful day. We basically kept to Jordan time, though in Syria. Did a quick tour of the Palmyra ruins, which in my opinion knock spots off Jerash[3] (*the Greco-Roman site in Jordan*), and then drove out to the tower tombs. These are really extraordinary, like Egypt's Valley of the Kings but all above ground. Then pressed on by main roads. This meant leaving Qasr al-Hayr East for another time -

perhaps we could spend the next winter vacation in Syria? Also didn't head directly north for Raqqa but going the long way via Deir ez-Zor.[4] A hell of a long and tedious desert drive to the Euphrates at Deir. Haven't been to this area before. Quite interesting. Desert much hotter than most of our part of Jordan. More like the south. Deir larger than expected but just as much a raw frontier town as expected. Since we'd been eating Norwegian buns all morning, and Freddie was full of biscuits, we skipped lunch and pressed on for Raqqa,[5] back up the Euphrates valley. This made for a long desert day, but got to Raqqa at about 5.15 p.m. local time. Found a very cheap local hotel (with cockroaches and used sheets) and got settled in. Colette and Freddie were still "settling" while I went off to see the Baghdad Gate.[6] The authorities must be putting a lot of money into restoration in Syria. I've seen photographs of what Qalaat Jaber[7] looks like now, and the walls of Raqqa have been virtually built to about fifteen feet high. Nothing like this last time I came here. Well done *(President)* Assad. Found a reasonable restaurant next door and had the same sort of food again (while Freddie leaked his nappy on a chair). It's still very much hotter here than expected, so we walked around a while, drank tea and bought some supplies before trying to get Freddie to sleep. That's when we found the cockroach. Colette freaked out! She takes these things very well these days - like her newfound ability to pee behind trees or even low rocks when necessary. Sat a while in the hotel and drank tea, plus "laban" = "ayran" offered by another guest.

Colette's version

Had to be up at 6.30 so that we could leave around 9. Only pitta bread, cheese, apricot jam and olives for breakfast and Freddie would eat only pitta bread and jam. We had left a water bottle with "ringe" (*orange drink*) in their fridge, so that it was ready for the Thermos now. Walked around Palmyra - impressive seeing those columns set against the desert hills. Walking in the sun, even with the strong wind, made me feel ill, so Freddie and I sat while David saw more. Drove across desert on a good road just under 300 kilometres. Very hot and tiring (*no air-conditioning in those days*). Let Freddie romp on desert sand for a bit and he didn't want to get back into the car. But I could see that in just a few minutes we are all getting burnt. Used all our juice and water, except for spare jug (non-drinking water) on roof-rack. Started to feel faint, but finally got to Deir ez-Zor. Tonic, ice-cream, biscuits, sweets. Freddie and I could eat and drink in public but David had to be very discreet (Ramadan). Too hot to have a meal per se, so drove to Raqqa, another 130 kilometres, where we found a scruffy but cheap hotel £3 ½. Decided not to put sponge on floor for Freddie when I saw a cockroach. So we used our sheet and pillows on my bed and Freddie slept with me. Far too hot, and I probably got 2-3 hours sleep.

Freddie and Colette playing ball in the remains of the medieval palace at Raqqa which, lying almost midway along the main caravan routes between the greater medieval cities of Damascus and Baghdad, was for a while the favourite city of Abbasid Caliphs who ruled an empire which stretched from the Atlantic to the frontier of China.

Stucco squinches and blind arches - matters of profound indifference to practically anyone except an aspiring academic who teaches the History of Islamic Art and Architecture. These fragments survive on the ruins of an early medieval Palace at Raqqa in north-eastern Syria.

The interior of the early medieval fortified wall of Raqqa. These massive mud-brick defences largely date from the early 9th century AD.

Although of strong gastronomic opinions, Freddie was nevertheless prepared to try most things; here a very crunchy piece of French bread in the city of Aleppo.

Sunday 17th June – Map: 3 Reyhanlı, Turkey

David's Version

A day that turned out to be harder than expected. Found all the main Raqqa sites in the morning and took too many photos. But probably worth it. Then off towards Aleppo. No sign of the Abu Hurayrah[8] minaret because we were on the new road, well away from Lake Assad. Did see a sign for the Meskene minaret, however, and so headed down a very dusty track and across dusty fields. Could see the minaret in the distance. What a setting! Right on the edge of the escarpment with the new lake below. Did they shift this minaret up from the valley? There seem to be some ruins down by the water's edge. Pressed on past the Syrian Air Force air college where Delfins[9] (silver) were doing circuits, into Aleppo. Got lost, found petrol but no place to change money. Got ripped off for a warm beer that I didn't want - they had nothing else - before finding a good pullup for Syrian lorry drivers. Here had a much better deal for lunch. Time getting on a bit now, so headed out for Deir Semaan.[10] This was a bit out of our way but was certainly worth the detour. Most impressive bit of late Roman stonework that I've ever seen. The frontier was only a short way away and we got through the Syrian side very easily indeed. But got a bit caught up on the Turkish border because we were behind a bus load of Turks. Also failed to get any car insurance (*for Turkey*). Time now very much against us, so drove into the nearest small town, Reyhanlı, and found a good small lokanta. Much more food variety here in Turkey compared to Syria or Jordan. Freddie got rice, which always goes down well. Next to a really seedy and cheap hotel. Very basic, but they did add a third bed to our room for Freddie. Took ages to fill all the passport forms, and Colette is obviously getting both very tired and very irritable. I hope to God tomorrow is easier, and the day after also. It's going to be a sweaty night. A young boy is leaning on this table, staring at my appalling handwriting.

Colette's Version

Drove from Raqqa to Aleppo. Then to Deir Semann (*Monastery*), then into Turkey, Reyhanlı.

Observations

Freddie seems to live on pitta bread (breakfast) and rice (supper). For supper his chair didn't fit in restaurant, so he stood on ordinary chair, but was too high. Moved his chair onto floor to stand on it, which was just the right height. "Beginning" to like spicey foods. Egg (hard boiled) sandwich for lunch with paprika in pitta bread of course, and he loved it. Fascinated by lizard at monastery, but scared of puppy in restaurant. Drinking so much juice (in some cases fizzy pop is all we can find), that he's getting shits again. But at least he's not getting dehydrated.

I keep drinking all day, but get a headache it seems even so. Can't take the heat! Stopped at scruffy hotel, with two beds and nothing else in room. They moved another bed in for Freddie and we pushed two of them together. Sink and toilet down corridor are <u>very</u> basic, but relatively clean. We had no choice, though, unless we pressed on. Got Freddie to bed at 9.30, too late to stop, but frontier held us up.

Oleanders, a milky blue reservoir and the Taurus Mountains as we drove up through the Cilician Gates from the Mediterranean coast to the interior plateau of Turkey.

Monday 18th June – Map: 4 Adana, Turkey

David's Version

Spent the whole day one hour out - being misled yesterday at the frontier. Anyway, thought we were up early. This hotel really was a bit rough, but then it only cost £2.50 a night for us three. Took it easy today, but still ended up reaching Adana a bit late. First to Antakya for car insurance (we managed to cover ourselves in Turkey but not Europe). Would have looked at the museum if Monday hadn't been the only day it shut. Pressed on to find Bagras castle.[11] This was a minor detour into a wonderful little green valley dominated by the castle perched on its isolated crag, and full of oleander and tiny fields. Quite idyllic. Colette was having tummy trouble but looked after Freddie in the village square, playing in the village fountain. Then pressed on a short way over the mountain to Iskenderun for a light lunch of shrimp omelette and beer. Next a very short hop to Payas which is down near the shore. The Ottoman fortress, mosque and hamam make a single complex. Very interesting and worthy of more time. Then back on the road for a short hop to Adana. Had a bit of trouble finding a reasonable hotel. I wanted to splash out, but nearly let a helpful local encourage me to splash a little too much. Colette restrained me, though I was so tired and sweaty that I began to get cross. She was right of course, and we ended up in a very nice, quite posh, and even *(not)* so quite expensive class three hotel. Cost as much as our last three nights together. Being on the sixth floor, with a Mrs. who can be quite forgetful, can get somewhat tiring. Anyway, all sorted out and went off for a very nice supper in a rather better place than usual. Still cheap, however. Now, while Colette does some laundry upstairs, I'm writing my diary, drinking a cold Efes beer and trying to plan the next stage of the journey. The bar lounge is full of Turks, all male, smoke and a badly dubbed TV version of the story of Gloria Vanderbilt. Wasn't she the original poor little rich girl?

Colette's Version

Got off to a good start, in fact had a better night's sleep. Now covered in mosquito bites. Didn't realise - should spray the room <u>every</u> night. To Antioch and then just as far as Adana where we stopped at a 3rd class hotel for about £15. What a treat. Rug (wall-to-wall) was clean to put down Freddie's sponge. Warm showers, laundry (not dry in morning so had to go in plastic bag).

Observations

Freddie's lunch consisted of rice and he wouldn't eat salad or omelette. Supper was rice and the potatoes from a stew. They're putting too much spice (paprika?) in the foods. We've now all had the shits, a regular thing for Turkey. Freddie won't drink fizzy pop (which is about all they seem to have in most places, Pepsi), but at least we've found an apricot nectar, watered down is just great for him. I started to have doubts about continuing when first I was constipated (pain!) and then got the shits with a vengeance. Feel better now.

Freddie pulling his mother into the mysterious interior of a rock-cut mosque rather than church at Göreme.

The painted interiors of the subterranean churches at Göreme range from the primitive and almost folksy, as seen here, to some of the finest examples of medieval Byzantine art.

For Freddie the troglodyte churches of Göreme[12] in Cappadocia were clearly less interesting than the huge ants which inhabited the area.

Tuesday 19th June – Map: 5 Ürgüp, Turkey

David's Version

A day I'd prefer to forget. I made a series of bad decisions and feared that I'd lose both Colette and the (forthcoming) baby. Anyway, to start. Awoke feeling hot and ropey. Put this down to the Adana climate. Drove north-east, having already shat my nappy, and reached Sis (the hilltop capital of the medieval kingdom of Cilician Armenia). This part of Cilicia is very fertile and beautiful, with the old Armenian capital in a very dramatic rocky-top position at the foot of a pass. And what a pass! The road was windy, fantastically beautiful, not improved by the fact that I felt like death, also running a temperature. Stopped at Feke for ayran (*plain yoghurt drink with some salt*). Felt better after this, so pressed on and, trying to cut some mileage, went across an absolutely incredible pass. A dirt track really. Colette getting into a panic about the baby and all the bumps. Me seriously considering putting her on a plane when and if ever we got over to the other side. She admitted she was frightened for the child, wept a little and was in considerable pain from the strain on the womb support ligaments. Eventually I had to ask to drive again, after we'd failed to find any food really suitable for Freddie at Develi. Got lost and added at least 20 kilometres. Eventually reached Ürgüp, found an acceptable hotel (Tepe Hotel, 4th class), had a few craps, which were hardly worthy of the name, being more like peeing out of the wrong orifice. Staggered into town to buy milk and juice, then fell mercifully into bed for a very feverish sleep.

Colette's Version

David not well (heat, recent diarrhoea, exhaustion?) so we got going later than expected. Why do I always perk up when David is not well? Long drive across Taurus Mountains. Had to decide whether to take longer route (at least twice) or shorter on a minor road. Chose latter, but what a mistake. Very rough - for a while thought we'd have to turn back. I ended up in tears, worrying that I would end up in early labour in the middle of nowhere. We then decided there would be no more detours. Got to Ürgüp around 9 pm, and found a 4th Class hotel. Tourist area in Cappadocia, £10 per night. David felt awful. Went to bed shortly after Freddie. Good night's sleep. Cool!

Wednesday 20th June – Map: 6 Ürgüp, Turkey

David's Version

Altogether a better day, mainly because Colette was happy and feeling great (and still talking to me, which I hardly deserved). Also because, although I still started out with the shits, I'd no temperature. Stayed in bed till twelve, while Freddie and Colette played with the hotel dogs, and with his football. Then to town. Day divided between site-seeing Cappadocian churches and abandoned troglodyte villages (carved from the soft rock of local cliffs), and pricing rugs. We should be able to get something good between £200 and £300 - next time, which will probably mean next year. Freddie loved climbing around the rock, in and out of the rock-cut churches, houses and so on. Colette liked the scenery, the climate (distinctly cooler) and the wall-paintings. She was also <u>very</u> keen on the carpets. Home for an early night, having failed (the only bum decision today) to get a delicate meal for my delicate tummy. Tried grilled river fish in Avanos. No taste at all, and four times as many tiny bones as any other member of the pisces genus. Must get some miles under our belt tomorrow.

Colette's Version

Slept later (8 a.m.) because David felt bloody. Terrible diarrhoea and sick feeling. Gave me a chance to do some laundry. Then Freddie and I had bread, jam and cheese. Restaurant kept our carton of milk in their fridge. Interesting - they had no milk of their own. In fact, wherever we go we ask them to put juice or whatever in fridge so it's ready for our thermos in a.m. (the following morning). David felt better and we saw a bit of Cappadocia in afternoon. Göreme and Zelme. Great place for children, as long as you watch that they don't fall off a cliff. After a while I was feeling weary, so we stopped for tea and then looked at carpets. Want to pay £200-£300 for a good one. Perhaps next trip back to London. Tiring day for Freddie and he slept in car all that time while we were in shop. Early night for everyone, as tomorrow is to be a long drive. Difficult to wash Freddie in cold water, and it didn't start warming up until 10 p.m. He screamed. Calamine lotion essential. Put it all over mosquito bites from other night. Baby Number 2 (*the future Antoinette*) kicking madly!

Thursday 21st June – Map: 7 Bolu, Turkey

David's Version

A day which should have been quite hard work, but otherwise straightforward, ended up as an unmitigated disaster. I really should never have tried this trip. It's altogether too ambitious, or I'm getting too old, or too stupid, or both. Perhaps I'm just getting tired. The day started off fine. We got away by 9.30 and had a pleasant, steady drive towards Ankara. The weather was clear and cool and the countryside much greener than I'd seen it before. Then, since we will hit the halfway mark tomorrow (in mileage), we decided to check and sort out our finances. Found ourselves very substantially short. It took the rest of the day heart-searching to work out that it was our four hundred dollars that had gone missing. Still don't know whether I left it at Irbid, gave to Colette who left it at Irbid, got robbed by a considerate thief who left me with another four hundred plus all my dinars, or simply gave it away, or what. Both now feeling totally depressed. Only Freddie is still perky. I'm truly regretting the whole trip and am sure the conference paper will be a farce (*which in the end David presented in French; see his diary entry for 5th July, nor did it prove to be a farce*). I'm just overconfident and overambitious, that's all. Also took an hour longer to reach Bolu than planned; the road had great stretches apparently under the plough, and the lorry traffic was as awful, as expected. The guide-book is, I am sure, quite wrong about the so-called Bayazit Mosque.[13] I'm sure they've got the wrong one as being by Bayazit (an early Ottoman sultan). It's the one next to the Orta Hamam (also by Bayazit). Anyway, we had a good, cheap supper of pizza then went through all the baggage looking for the missing money. Failed, of course. So am now stuck in a smoke-filled, Turk-filled room, drinking (one) coffee, and looking at a TV programme about the Istanbul music-hall scene in the 1920s. What disasters will tomorrow bring?

Colette's Version

Drove all day on a busy road, loads of lorries, through Ankara and as far as Bolu on our way to Istanbul. David feeling much better. We must have driven 300 miles and my back started to hurt. Kept changing position and used pillow behind lower back. Lovely soup for lunch and Freddie wanted rice. He also wanted rice for supper but also had some of my different sort of pizza. Maybe too much rice in tummy is a good thing for him - not a lot of oil as he would get from meat or potato stews. Hotel under £5 - not bad. Both lunch and supper were under £1 each. Good thing as we have just discovered that we've either lost or left behind $400 that we had changed. We're both feeling ill at the thought, but know the trip must go on.

Darkened interiors such as that of the Kadi Timurtash Mosque in Bolu held no fear for young Freddie, in fact they were an enticing source of adventure.

As we journeyed across central Turkey, Freddie discovered that his favourite food was rice - any time of day! Fortunately, the small local lokantas or restaurants which we frequented rarely failed to produce what the young man demanded, in this case in the town of Bolu.

Friday 22nd June – Map: 8 Lüleburgaz, Turkey

David's Version

No disasters but a deal of depression and a bad scare. Up early to look around Bolu. Found it shrouded in fog, plus smoke from Bayazit's bath-house next door. The E5 *(main road)* from here to Istanbul was simply awful. Crowded, polluted, half under construction, dangerous, slow, and not much fun either. Staggered into Istanbul well behind schedule but found the Kariye Camii very easily. Had a very nice and restful "chay" (*Turkish tea*) next to the church (cheap too). The mosaics and above all the paintings were superb and well worth the detour. Unfortunately, had to press on, spirits still low, for wherever we could get to. Had hoped to get into Bulgaria but ended up at

Lüleburgaz. Stopped first at Corlu in the hope of changing money. In fact the banks were shut, but in the process we thought we'd left the passports in Bolu! Colette nearly had genuine hysterics. Again it was my fault because, in the morning rush, I'd kept them in my pocket instead of giving them to her, and had then taken off my jacket, in the heat of the day, throwing it onto the back seat. Next to Lüleburgaz, found hotel but had no money for supper. Then a young agricultural engineer, speaking better French than I, offered to stake us until the banks opened. In the event the hotel changed some dollars for us, but we still had a nice supper with this chap and, after I'd helped put Freddie down, I went off for a beer with him. Also looked around the big mosque and caravanserai complex in the centre of town. Very impressive. Altogether a pleasant evening, though inevitably the conversation got around to modern sexual morality. All in French too! It basically boiled down to telling him not to believe that the "West" was really like the TV shows.

Colette's Version

Drove all day on a horrid road (E5), full of crazy lorries and thought we could have reached Istanbul by lunchtime. Roadworks and traffic put us behind schedule by about four hours, and we had to stop yet another night in Turkey. Hadn't changed enough money, so a nice young Turk, also staying at the hotel, paid for our supper and we'll pay back in a.m. when we've been to the bank. Again Freddie wanted rice at lunch and supper, but he managed to also eat a fair amount of Kofte Kebab. Freddie and I both have a dose of the "Turkey Trots". Difficult to keep a balance between starving this out of my system and eating enough to keep up my strength.

The Great Khan at Lüleburgaz in Turkish Thrace tends to be overlooked by foreign visitors, as does most of European Turkey except Istanbul itself. It is nevertheless one of the finest examples of 16th century Ottoman secular architecture, designed, like so much from this period, by the great Sinan.

The Mehmet Paşa Mosque in Lüleburgaz was also designed by Sinan's team, completed in 1549 and further adorned by a very large stork's nest on top of the main dome.

Saturday 23rd June – Map: 9 Tolbuhin [now Dobrich], Bulgaria

David's Version

Another bad day, though not as bad as some. Started off pleasantly with a wander around the caravanserai with Colette and Freddie, then to the frontier (with Bulgaria), further and slower than expected. No trouble there, except that (*travel*) insurance cost $19, which was a bit steep, then it rained like hell in the mountains. Couldn't find any place to have lunch until 4.30 (what a country! no cafes or such, nothing like Turkey). Couldn't find "super" petrol (advisable even for a Fiat Panda in Bulgaria) until we reached Varna, and nowhere would take a Super-Coupon for an Ordinary Benzine equivalent. What a system - even when they would get the advantage. What would the "system" have done if I'd simply run out on the road? Towns dismal and surrounded by "workers' flats", people generally surly. You really have to work to get a smile-response. Tried to find a snack at a kind of mini-coastal resort. Ended up with ice-cream from a stall where the lady simply ignored a whole line of children with their pennies while she talked to some young man. Also four excellent sweet fluffy pancakes. Lunch-cum-supper of sausage, salad and beer was very good, but the price was ludicrous. Nineteen dollars!!! Didn't have enough Bulgarian leva so the fellow was kind enough to take all that I had, let me off the last two and left me flat broke in Bulgarian. Colette freaked again and tore him off a strip. Eventually decided to stop at Tolbuhin. A real modern, high-rise hell-hole of a dump. Totally impersonal and characterless centre to it. Fortunately got pounced on by two black-market sharks and changed some money at twice the official rate. The main (and only official for foreigners) hotel was too pricey, but these guys took me to an old one in the process of restoration. Gone so long that Colette was about to call the police. But booked in, paid up and settled down. Miles from the nearest parking place of course, since this is a "pedestrian town". While I was gone on one occasion, someone tried to pull Colette into the gents' toilet. She was very upset when I got back, but settled down. No milk available for Freddie but the large and jolly lady proprietress showed us how to find and then mix yoghurt and sugar with water. Freddie seems to like it. No food or tea either. Come to think of it, not much fun at all. Incidentally, our room is being used as a store during repairs and is crammed with spare furniture.

Colette's Version

Got to Bulgarian frontier and made our way up the coastal road and then inland to Tolbuhin. First time we used side curtains to keep sun off Freddie. Took much longer to drive here than expected. Couldn't find a restaurant until 5.30, and then it cost us

$17 for two sausages, salad, one beer, orange drink, water and bread. I blew my top and told man his prices were too high and that we had no money left to sleep. It's the communist system that apparently sets these prices so I feel bad now that I blamed him. Couldn't find a petrol station for miles that sold super; we had a coupon that was good only for 10 litres of it. Got to Tolbuhin and had no more Bulgarian money left. As David went to look at a hotel (which would probably take dollars), two guys on black market said they'd change some. Gave us a much better exchange, then showed David a cheaper hotel under renovation. Our room full of furniture, but comfortable. One third the price of the other. While David went to get more luggage, a fellow tried to seduce me (I think!) and I managed to lock the door behind me. Fell apart when David got back. Freddie wanted milk and manageress brought us to restaurant where we got yoghurt to mix with water and sugar. It was good and he drank it. Saw "fellow" working in the restaurant.

Sunday 24th June – Map: 10 Călărași, Romania

David's Version

An odd and very mixed day. Got out of Tolbuhin, despite an unfinished spaghetti junction on the outskirts. Easy to the frontier and easy out of Bulgaria. Incidentally, breakfast in a workers' cafeteria, cheap and included ham and inferior orange juice. No choice really. Getting into Romania was friendly, courteous and extremely thorough. They search just about everything. Took almost two hours at the frontier. Had to change large numbers of dollars, but again done in a friendly and sympathetic way. Seem to have avoided insurance altogether (for Romania). Not necessarily a good thing, however. Anyway, almost lunchtime by the time we pressed on. Had good directions from frontier police to get to Adamklissi. This has been totally reconstructed. Total effect distinctly odd, courtesy of Chairman Ceaucescu. I only hope it's an accurate reconstruction. But impressive. Colette feeling headachy and altogether rough. Freddie very hungry. Car short of benzine. Getting desperate when everything near the monument and in village proved to be shut. Then a supposed officer of a group of soldier-tourists suggested we follow him to the next door cooperative farm. The young lady who worked at the monument, and who spoke excellent "English" English - via the BBC Course surely - came too. Followed these two, who rode in a donkey cart, to a farm. Quite an experience and a real eye-opener for Colette. Had a fine lunch, while Freddie consumed all the potatoes in sight. Next pressed on to the map-signed petrol station. Shut. Used spare can on roof. Also had a puncture, so no spare tyre or petrol left. Reach Danube at Orsova. Dribbling rain. Awaited ferry, bought half a kilo of cherries and chatted in German (sort of) with a heating control engineer who'd worked in Syria. Only drove to the next town, Călăraşi. Found super benzine which was a distinct improvement on Bulgaria. Next found the hotel. High class, expensive, and to hell with it. We deserve it by now and anyway each foreigner has to exchange US dollars a day (*the exact amount was omitted from this diary; however, this was part of the rules for tourism in several eastern European countries in those days*). So we've got to use it somehow. Colette in a very frail state by now. Decided against eating in the place on assumption it would be expensive. Searched around town, and found a restaurant-cum-disco. Only thing there was. Noisy, lively, and some fun. Had wine and mineral-water, ate an excellent meal for a moderate price (not particularly cheap, but it did include wine, fruit juice for Freddie, excellent service by a jolly young lady, and a live band). Freddie had a ball. Danced and got "chatted up" by Romanian girls who were really too old for him, being at least two or three. I wept a bit, partly because I saw myself in Freddie, and hoped he'd avoid my sillier errors (sexually and in other ways – *namely, a near complete lack of confidence with women until I met Colette who changed everything*), and because

Colette had cheered up after hours of being down. Back at the hotel, I left them to get each other to sleep. While I write my diary I find that the place has largely died on its feet by quarter to eleven.

You can have hours of fun squirting water from a tap on a very hot day, which was just as well as we were stuck on the Bulgarian-Romanian frontier for bloody hours!

Colette's Version

Tolbuhin.

Couldn't find milk, don't think they use it here! Workmen's caf for breakfast. Freddie would eat only cake. We had a nice change with a small piece of ham or bacon, but rolls were stale. Spent ages at frontier but finally got into Romania. Feels "Latin", a nice change. Still couldn't find an open restaurant (Sunday or always?) and after visiting Adamklissi were invited back to co-op farm for soup, bread, beans and bacon. Lucky break that girl at monument spoke good English. Left Freddie's fork behind (*this was an important christening present, as I remember, so very sad to lose it – though it was later returned by these kind people*)!! I must have looked very hungry and weak, but that's what pregnancy does. Stayed the night at quite a nice hotel in Călărași ($27 inc. breakfast). Too posh really, but it was getting late and we had no choice. Afraid to use the restaurant, so found one outside, which turned out to be a disco. Freddie had a great time, flirting and dancing with a little girl. Too late for him to go to bed, but it was fun.

The huge monument at Adamklissi is supposed to be a faithful replica of the Tropaeum Traiani built in 109 AD to commemorate the Roman Emperor Trajan's victory over the Dacians. Freddie was decidedly impressed.

PS. With so much driving I've learned to hold my stomach wherever it looks bumpy ahead. It helps ease the strain. Pillows too.

In those days Romania had just about the worst government in the Soviet bloc, but also some of the nicest and most interesting people, including the young lady guide at Adamklissi. Unfortunately, Freddie was tired and "in a mood" by the time she took us to Collective Farm Number One where we nevertheless had a splendid lunch courtesy of the farmers.

Getting off the Danube ferry on the northern side of the river. Freddie is actually wearing one of his last proper nappies but Colette is bravely hiding her terror at running out of these vital essentials.

On the ferry across the broad Danube with the less than scenic city of Călăraşi in the background. Freddie still sports the ultimate pudding basin haircut while David's Tintin quiff is back.

Though David did not yet realise it, he already had the daughter he really wanted. This little Romanian-Wallachian costume doll, also bought on the frontier, would be amongst the first in Antoinette's ever-expanding collection of special dolls.

Monday 25th June – Map: 11 Donji Milanovac, Yugoslavia [now Serbia]

David's Version

A day definitely to forget. Began by wandering around Călăraşi trying to find nappies. Failed to the degree that, when I got one of our surviving specimens out to explain what I needed, I attracted a crowd, five deep all round, some of whom started flashing money and saying how much did I want for the nappy! Went to a few shops but only wasted time. Decided to head for Bucharest. Got there in the pissing rain and, after meeting assorted helpful people, failed utterly to get nappies. Colette now desperate and worried since we only had two left. Clearly it was impossible to travel in Romania with a baby, so said goodbye to the idea of the Moldavian churches and headed hard for the Yugoslav border, getting more depressed by the mile. Got horribly detoured and then hopelessly lost because of a damn dam scheme. Had to queue for petrol at the next stage and then drive into the night, reach the frontier at gone 11 o'clock. As there was a queue, chose to go back to the nearest town *(this was Orşova, though I neglected to write that at the time)* for a hotel. This was hugely expensive and one of the porters tried to diddle with a hardly any cheaper room in the basement as long as we were out by 6 o'clock - with a baby! So back to the frontier. Here the authorities relented and gave us a very easy time. Eventually changed most of our money and petrol coupons back - at a discount - *(petrol had to be pre-purchased in the form of coupons to ensure that western visitors paid more for their fuel than the local inhabitants)* and bought a souvenir with the remainder (a very colourful, embroidered serviette or small table-cloth). Found a good and reasonably priced modern hotel just on the other side in Yugoslavia, and crashed out with total relief *(this was in the town of Donji Milanovac)*.

Though lacking nappies, Romania boasted tourist souvenirs which were actually worth having. This woven cloth was purchased to use up otherwise non-exchangeable currency at the frontier.

Colette and Freddie displaying their triumphal find having re-crossed the Danube into what was then Yugoslavia. In fact, Freddie is wearing the very last of the Pampers as a treat after a day in a sodden towel stolen from a hotel.

Colette's Version

No milk in restaurant. No juice. They say that shops don't open until 12, and tea or lemonade is all they can give Freddie. We had bread and butter and marmalade after a long wait in a disorganised restaurant. Then tried to find nappies (we're down to two!). Babies in communist countries don't wear nappies. David got out of car. Nowhere to be found! Pressed on to Bucharest. No nappies. Friendly Romanian woman with good English directed us to a department store which suggested towels. Lady said she had babies and used "black market" nappies from abroad. Pressed on for Yugoslavia to find nappies and arrived at frontier at 11 p.m. Thought at first we'd stay at hotel on Romanian side but it was $41 a night! Told we could stay in servants' quarters for a bit cheaper but we'd have to be out by 6 a.m. No way! So back to frontier where they let us through very quickly. Freddie has been wearing a towel round him all day. Very embarrassing when, obviously very wet and bulky, we stopped for supper. Didn't seem to bother him, he still seems quite happy. Money that frontier wouldn't change we used on a couple of souvenirs, tablecloth and Romanian doll *(which was subsequently given to Antoinette)*. Drove into Yugoslavia and reached a hotel (posh for $20 per night, half Romanian price) with breakfast at 1 a.m. Clocks change though, so it's only midnight! (*Donji Milanovac, the Lepenski Vir hotel, dating from 1972 and hence quite new*)

PS. The reason I'm using red pen is that woman in small shop in Călărași gave me cotton pantaloons for Freddie as a "cadeau" and then asked me for my black Bic pen, which I gave her as a "cadeau".

People kept asking us throughout Communist countries for cigarettes, or for magazines from England, and even nappies.

When we were looking in Călărași, David jumped out of car with one in his hand to ask a lady carrying baby what she put on her baby. She couldn't understand, of course, and soon a crowd surrounded David five deep, pulling out wallets and asking to buy some! I wish I had the courage to photograph it.

Tuesday 26th June – Map: 12 Belgrade, Yugoslavia [now Serbia]

David's Version

Slightly better day, though far from perfect. Lay in a while then had a gentle breakfast. Freddie and even Colette had bounced back from yesterday. Failed again with nappies but changed a little money. No petrol coupons yet. Followed the Derdap Danube Gorge, which was stupendous, as far as the next castle. By now had coupons, more money and some rather inadequate Balkan versions of disposable nappies, which made everyone feel better. Well on the way to Belgrade when had <u>another</u> puncture - and no spare, since my energies had been focussed on nappy problems. A French family stopped and took me, plus two wheels, to the next town which was very close. Got tyres mended and back on the road within half an hour. Amazing! Everyone very helpful. Now to Belgrade. Hotels at first very expensive and full. Thought we had another disaster on our hands but Colette suggested the railway station area. Did so and got a place (Class C) for a very high price, but none the less a place. Colette again depressed, but cleaned Fred, went out, bought some plastic pants and found a very cheap and cheery local restaurant. Good grub and good beer. People very friendly. Made me feel better anyhow. They were all over Freddie of course. I suspect we are in the red light area. Too many women just hanging around. Also sad student travellers who can't afford these hotels. Strongly advised to take stuff off roof of car and, as this time this coincided with my instincts, I did so. Wait for the morrow to see if anything is left (sponge for seat still on roof), inside or out. Italian youngsters (ragazzi) squatting dismally outside hotel in the drizzle, asking me where I was going. They'll have the bloody wheels off, given half a chance.

Colette's Version

Nice sleep last night and we had a bit of a well-deserved lie-in. Found Freddie rice and gravy at breakfast! Looked for nappies. None. Told to try Belgrade, so after changing $20 at the hotel because the bank wouldn't change money until 12, we started driving. Passed by a beautiful gorge, Derdap Gorge, the same name as the hotel we had stayed at. Then stopped to change money, get petrol coupons and <u>look for nappies</u>! Found only what looked like large ladies' sanitary napkins, but made for baby, along with plastic pants that were too large. Bought forty of them but I'm having to use two at a time. Hasn't solved the problem, only eased it. Stopped for lunch along the lake on the Danube, then had <u>another</u> flat tyre. David had been so preoccupied with solving this nappy problem that he hadn't yet had tyre fixed from the flat a couple of days ago. Thank goodness for a French couple who took him into the nearest town with both tyres. Luckily the town was just a couple of kilometres away. Needed to wait only about half hour. Pushed on to Belgrade where we had to pay £24 ($32) for a night in a class C hotel, the expense is worrying but with a baby and short sleep last night we didn't have any choice. Made up for expense by having supper in what seemed a workmen's café - chips, beer and wiener schnitzel. Also looked for proper Pampers (*good quality disposable nappies*), but found only another pair of tighter fitting plastic pants. Used towel from hotel as night-time nappy. Freddie has been very good through all this - as happy as a clam.

Still using sponge on floor - a great success as long as the place looks clean. Sheet and extra blanket we're carrying too.

Wednesday 27th June – Map: 13 Vrbovsko, Yugoslavia [now Croatia]

David's Version

Thank god for a good day, with no disasters, well not really. Not very exciting, however. Got up early. Had a first-rate breakfast, found the car hadn't been rifled, failed to find nappies in Beograd's (*Belgrade's*) main pharmacy and headed off down that other "hell road" towards Zagreb. Not that it's so bad, compared to others we are now used to. Made regular stops for coffee, nappy changes, and a first-class fish soup lunch and yet more coffee. But tedious and surprisingly warm. Found myself having extended and detailed erotic fantasies about Janice (*a friend of Colette's*)! I think I must be getting a bit hungry. Yugoslav petrol coupons didn't buy much petrol, and since they are in face-value denominations rather than litres, this can be very misleading. Anyway, fantasies and benzine problems aside, it was a very boring journey to Zagreb. Thence headed south-west towards Rijeka. Pressed on past Karlovac into delightful hills and forests and valleys. Very green and sub-Alpine. Failed to find small guesthouses, so stopped at a Motel with a stupendous view. Terrified of what the cost would be, but pleasantly surprised. Had another excellent meal here, at a good price. The only dampener, which was more of a joke by now, was that the manager reported that yet another (the third) of my tyres had gone flat. It's a conspiracy! Changed it before got too dark and then settled down to drink a large draught beer, write a letter to Farm Number One at Adamklissi hoping to get Freddie's little fork back (Colette having left it in Romania) and writing up this so-called diary. It must be the most boring journal ever written. Hoping for some nooky tonight but I doubt it will happen.

Colette's Version

Found no nappies in Belgrade. Funny how ladies in pharmacies so far have been very unhelpful and unfriendly! Got on horrid road from Belgrade to Zagreb, loads of lorries, and made me a nervous wreck. We're putting Freddie to bed too late! Found a lovely hotel (£8) in Vrbovsko on the way to Rijeka. Now it's easy to find milk. Sponge on floor poses a problem when Freddie moves a lot in his sleep. Found him crying under our bed! Still using those "sanitary towel" type nappies, but they're now working better with tighter plastic pants. I reckon they cost 75p a day though (£5 over a week as opposed to £10 in Jordan), since I have to use two at a time.

The green and pleasant view of Vrbovsko from the motel.

What a happy pair! At a motel in the sunny uplands
of Vrbovsko in what was then north-western Yugoslavia, now Croatia.

Thursday 28th June – Map: 14 Trieste, Italy

David's Version

A better day, I think. Though full of decisions. The main one being that I'll never try another trip like this with children. It's just not practical. Could have been up and away early except that had to go to bank and the hotel misdirected me. Anyway, on road by ten through beautiful green, wooded and hilly scenery. Thence down to Rijeka, which began to look very Austro-Hungarian and even a little Italian. Stopped for coffee and cake ("tort") just the other side of a splendid hotel overlooking the sea. Should have cost a bomb, but didn't. It was a bit like the Villa Rosa at Camogli (*where, as a young teenager, I had spent two holidays with my parent*s), with the sea a sheer drop from the balcony. Was an old Austrian rich family home pre-1918. Not Hotel Astoria but a lot like it. Freddie loved "tort". Pressed on to Pula, having trouble finding a place for lunch. Ended up very cheap and good. Pula a let-down, not because of the place, which is fine, scenic and with a splendid amphitheatre, but because the carving I was looking for wasn't in the Archaeological Museum as I'd read. Pushed on north again, behind schedule and pissed off. Reached Poreč, though had thought of ditching it. Glad didn't. Like a mini-Dubrovnik. Pedestrianised, full of character and tourists. Church and mosaics both worth the visit. Stone mosaics outside very reminiscent of Madaba and Mount Nebo. Also terrific ice-cream, but expensive. But sod it! Now well behind time so went flat out for Trieste. Huge relief to reach Italy. Skies grey and full of rain. Found small restaurant and apparently small hotel without much trouble. Food as welcoming as the people, making us feel well and truly into the West. But not cheap, or I have got the exchange rate wrong. Hotel far from cheap, but it was now raining. We're tired, glad to be here, and not inclined to go searching around. It's also late. Got thoroughly soaked while bringing our normal excessive amount of baggage up to the fourth floor. Went for a walk, got lost, rained on again, back to original restaurant-bar for beer and diary writing. Lots of noise, laughter and cheeriness. I wonder how much this beer (a "grandi") will cost. Came to 2000 lira. Colette not pleased with the drink I bought her. She really is hard to please these days.

The great Roman arena or amphitheatre in Pula is one of the best preserved in the world.

Freddie's very first ice-cream, at Poreč in what is now Croatia.

Colette's Version

Freddie is very fussy today. He needs more sleep, although he's napping quite a bit during the day. We seem to be doing a lot of driving every day, but we haven't had another promised two days break yet. I need it - laundry is mounting, no launderette around, I'm too tired in evening to do it and very little place in hotels to hang it anyway. Drove today to peninsula of Istria, like Italian Riviera but probably cheaper, yes I'm sure it is. Down to Pula, and up to Trieste, where we found rice for Freddie, egg plant parmesan and noodles, plus a very overpriced hotel (about £13) again though it was almost 9 p.m. and it was raining, so we had little choice. The sore on Freddie's face has now flared up again (heat, sweat?), and I've put Vaseline (which didn't do much), then Betnovate ointment and I'll hope for the best. Some heartburn today - what did I eat? Fish soup with paprika yesterday.

Essentials in Car

Paper towels, washing up liquid, toilet rolls (2), loads of nappies, soap, towels (wet one in car in a plastic bag, wash every day), thermos flasks (2), bottle brush, Tommy Tippee *(child's spill-proof drinking cup with a lid)*, drinking water, washing water, and juice concentrates, potty and disinfectant, flip flops, Raid *(insect killing aerosol)*, washing powder, calculator (for estimating costs), sponge sheet for Freddie's bed on floor.

The Euphrasian Basilica in Poreč might be a jewel of Byzantine civilization, but on a hot and very humid day even the ever-patient Colette can start to feel that her husband asks too much.

Mosaics in the apse of the Euphrasian Basilica at Poreč, Croatia, are amongst the most beautiful examples of early Byzantine art in the central Mediterranean.

Friday 29th June – Map: 15 Venice, Italy

David's Version

Altogether a better day, though with a few problems. Took it easy in the morning. Failed to change Jordanian dinars anywhere. Began to panic till I remembered the good old Eurocard. So straight to Banco di Napoli and got equivalent of £50. Next stop nappies. Your actual Pampers! The real McCoy. Then a roll of film for me, and so packed up, paid up and buggered off. Day really grey and dismal. Had pissed with rain last night. Anyway, reached Acquileia at 12.15, quarter of an hour after the church shut until 3 o'clock. Decided to hang about, so got permission to photograph in the crypt from the Directorate Office, had a beer and then walked into the village for lunch. This was good but very expensive. Also bought a book, some slides and a toy car (Fiat Panda) for Freddie. I realised that this little exercise would make our easy and early day somewhat less so, but seemed important enough. In fact the frescoes in the Basilica were well worth it. Some really interesting stuff down there, in addition to my supposed "Hungarian" archer. Met an Italian who was interested in later Italian military uniforms, who also thought the archer was probably Hungarian. Next decided to press on hard down the Autostrada for Venice. Rained like the devil, but still got to Mestre by 5.15. Took our time to find a pensione. Ended up at a locanda for 3,000 lire per night, very near the station. The cheapest and the most convenient. Quite a lively little town. I did most of the laundry because Colette was having nasty pelvic pains. Even found a place to hang the wet clothes on the roof, though I had to remake and retrieve a few abandoned clothes pegs from the ledge of the roof. Thence for supper at the cheapest "Tourist menu" available. Excellent grub, moderate price but appallingly slow service. But all more cheerful than for several days. If we can change some more money tomorrow, I think I'd like to stay here for three nights (2 days).

The Basilica at Aquileia where David was once again hunting wall-paintings.

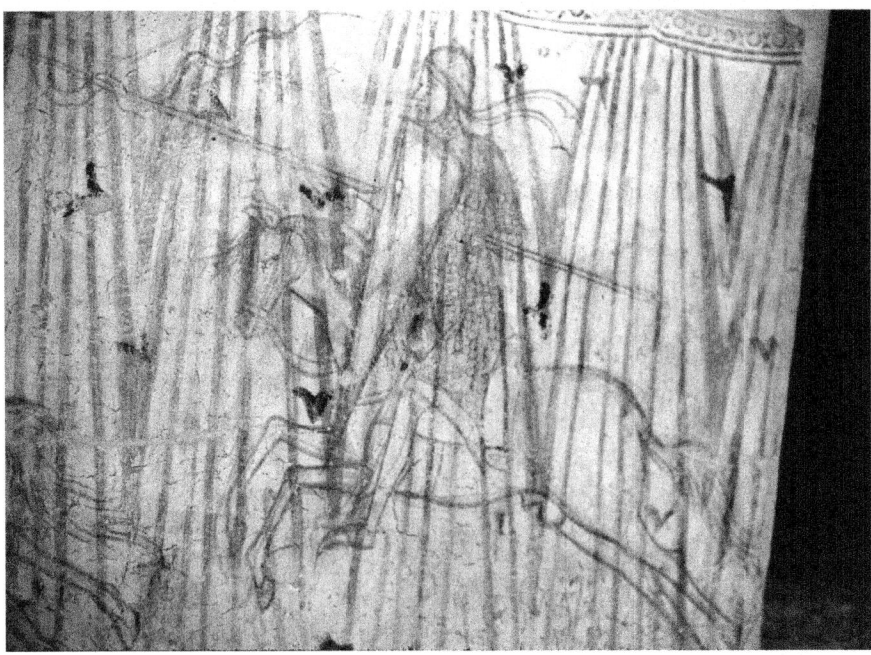

These wall paintings in the Crypt of Massenzio beneath the Basilica of Aquileia date from the 12th century and are made to look like textile wall-hangings. The knight pursuing a mounted archer could represent a Crusader and a Saracen, or a battle against Magyar (Hungarian) raiders.

Colette's Version

Better sleep last night (we're in Trieste), although hotel is more expensive than I wanted to pay in Italy (about £12). No bank would cash our Jordanian dinars, so I cashed a cheque for £50 using Barclaycard. Looks like this is what we'll have to do for rest of trip and then change our 400 JD when we get to London. Found Pampers (!) and bought sixty of them. Found that they cost about 9p each compared to 10p in Jordan, so they're not even expensive!!! Drove to Acquileia and had to wait almost three hours for crypt to open so David could see frescoes. Stayed in locanda in Mestre near Venice. Pizzeria for supper and from "Tourist Menu" Freddie had some of my tagliatelli and chips. He's eating mostly carbohydrates now. Must remember to give vitamins every day (I forgot today). Big laundry day, but David did most of it as I got a terrific pain in pelvis. Clothes-line up on our roof - a great bonus!

Saturday 30th June – Map: 16 Venice, Italy

David's Version

Our "Venice day" turned out tiring but satisfactory, but with one major crisis. Up and away quite early. Good Italian coffee and croissant breakfast then train to Venice then "bus" down the Grand Canal. Found an exchange place after discovering that the banks, contrary to information in Mestre, were shut on Saturday morning. All going well until the man in charge discovered that Colette had a Visa rather than a Eurocheque card. So no exchange even with cheques. Near hysterics as I had a Eurocard but my chequebook was still in the car in Mestre. Stupid of me and no excuse. So I left them two in St. Mark's Square (without any money) while I hurried back to Mestre. Walked to the rail station to save both money and time. Same on way back. Took opportunity of a few pics. Sweating like hell and hour and a half later back at San Marco. But did get some money now! Late for lunch and Freddie about to sleep, so headed for SS Giovanni e Paolo. Ice-cream on the way, which is hard to eat from a small tub while carrying a baby in one arm. Rest of the day moderately restful tourism. Doge's Palace, St. Mark's, etc., though even this was very hard on Colette. Good for the old art-slides (*35 mm transparencies*) though (I hope). Took water bus up Grand Canal as far as San Toma then walked to the Friary area. There we had a good supper. Freddie ate exceptionally well and even walked - indeed ran - almost all the way thence to the rail station. Freddie had a sudden emergency crap just as we crossed the Canal to the station, but this crisis over, my primary concern was once again Colette who was, by now, absolutely flaked out. Quiet coffee in a bar then back to bed for Freddie. Now I'm again writing this foolish diary in the same bar as last night. It seems largely to be run by, and be frequented by, women. The few men around seem to be on sufferance. But there's lots of room and good soft chairs.

Colette's Version

Coffee and filled croissant for breakfast, then found we couldn't cash a cheque in Mestre but bank was open in San Marco Square. It wasn't! Money exchange wouldn't take my cheque without EC (*Eurocheque*) card and all I had was Barclaycard. David had card but had left his chequebook in car back at Mestre. He had to go back; I panicked because I had key to room and thought chequebook was there. Near hysterics and many tears as I raced to no avail to catch him before he left on vapore (*the canal bus*). Only one woman stopped to try and help me because she thought I had lost my "bambino". Calmed down. Freddie played with pigeons and seemed happy. David got back and changed £100. Freddie liked pizza and lasagne for lunch. Supper - extra bowl of rice for him was not necessary and very costly - put meal up by about 5000 lire (£2). Good idea to bring bottle or thermos of juice while walking around. Too expensive to stop in café every time he wants a drink. Tourist Menu a good idea to give him a fair choice of eats.

It's called pizza. Freddie and his father enjoy a little of the local cucina outside the Scuola Grande di San Marco in Venice. Of course, David was actually there to see the medieval tombs in the Basilica of San Giovanni e Paolo next door.

Freddie, meanwhile, thought the Venetian pigeons the funniest things he had seen in weeks.

Freddie and a small canal somewhere in Venice.

Venice brought a smile back to her face, as it should.

Sunday 1st July – Map: 17 Parma, Italy

David's Version

The only "disaster" today, apart from things being missing or shut, was a growing terror about money. We are getting through it at an alarming rate here in Italy. Anyway, up and away at a good hour. Had almost cleared Mestre when Freddie threw up. His tum's clearly not quite right at the moment. In fact he hardly ate all day until a very late supper. So on to Padua. Appallingly complicated city with quite unintelligible one-way systems and very few signposts. Got to the Gattemelata statue OK, and Colette took Freddie for part of a mass in the St. Anthony (of Padua) Basilica next door. Thence drove quite literally in circles about three times to find the Arena Chapel, which was shut. My information about the San Guistina Church and its carvings was all up the pole, so failed to find these at all. Most of the day gone by the time we cleared Padua, having had a ludicrously expensive plate of pasta on the way - £7 for two plates of pasta, a Coke and a mineral water!! So pissed off that almost decided to head direct for Parma and Tiziana's (*an Italian friend working with me at Yarmouk University in Jordan*) parents' place. In the end stuck to the original plan. Ferrara as good as last time. The castle still impressive and the Cathedral front is most impressive. Good carvings too. The inside has been totally, but tastefully, Baroquified. This time had a hugely expensive beer and orange-juice, plus a splendid small bun - £2. Getting rather down in the mouth by the time we reached Bologna. It looked expensive, so pressed on to Parma in the hope of finding Tiziana. Tried phoning on the way a few times, but couldn't get through. Had a rather steep, light supper in an autostrada pull-up. Nearly lost over £1 here in an effort to phone again. Reached Parma and were immediately told that Tiziana's parents live in a tiny village up in the hills about twenty kilometres away. So gave up hope of a free night and instead drove round Parma in increasing desperation, looking for a cheap hotel. Failed.

Ended up in a quite nice 3rd class place, which was a bit more expensive than last night. It does, however, have a bar, though I'm getting nervous about asking the price of this beer.

The striking bronze statue of the condottiero Erasmo di Narni, nicknamed Gattemelata, is one of Donatello's finest works. It overlooks the Piazza del Santo in Padua.

Colette's Version

Decided to leave after two nights instead of three. I'm getting very tired. Travelling has been going on too long and yesterday was no rest. We left for Padua and Freddie and I went to Mass in St. Anthony's Basilica as David took photos (Freddie threw up five minutes outside Mestre. Good he hadn't had too much milk!) Very frustrating for him (David), as one-way streets made it near impossible to find what he wants and then when we got there it was shut. Found that at the end of today we had only £12 left of the £100 changed yesterday. Whatever happened to cheap holidays in Italy? Went to Ferrara and then to Parma, where we hoped to see Cliffino and Tiziana. No answer on phone. So we got hotel (another £14!). This is getting ridiculous. We can't find cheap places, or is it that we're so restricted with Freddie. We had our ups and downs today, getting depressed about money and the fact that we're not having a good time. This trip has turned into a chore, but we had to press on and try to keep up morale and economise. Maybe more gelati is the answer.

"Dad shows me some good stuff"; father and son with a 12th century stone griffin crushing a chariot pulled by unhappy oxen outside the Basilica at Ferrara.

The fearsome carved griffins may have been impressive, but Freddie found a cold fountain in Ferrara that was much more suitable on a day like this.

Monday 2nd July – Map: 18 Fino Mornasco [Como], Italy

David's Version

An altogether better day, though the way we spend money is terrifying. We seem to be averaging £50 per day since Istanbul. Enjoyed Parma, met an Italian girl from Berkshire behind the counter in the breakfast place, and one from Kingsbury behind the counter in an ice-cream shop. Found a splendid (carved) capital covered in knights in the Cathedral, though didn't have the kit to photograph it. Get permission for next time. Mended spare tyre, filled with petrol, including spare can. So all set up and raring to go, headed for Fidenza. Even found some new armoured warriors here. I'm coming towards a theory that the Italians were the first in Western Europe to adopt the separate mail coif, judging with the number of mail hauberks shown without coifs at all. Almost a disaster here as Colette dropped Freddie's new shorts (*matching Harvard University tank-top*), the ones from Madeleine *(Colette's sister),* and got very upset about it. But walked back and found that someone had picked them up and put them safe on a window-sill. Next stop Pavia which has a magnificent "Historic Centre". All these are worthy of much more time. Saw two nice Romanesque churches, had an ice-cream and pressed on. Lots of today has been on Autostradas, which pushes up the cost, not to mention expensive fruit, a large chunk of Parmesan cheese and a fair amount of ice-cream. And so towards Como and the Swiss frontier. Stopped short at a small village *(almost certainly Fino Mornasco, though it was not written in the diary)* a few miles from Como and found a much cheaper locanda next to the railway station and a level-crossing. I expect a noisy night. Also had what I hope will be a moderately priced meal (risotto and shared portions of ham and melon, plus beers). We'll see. Now I'm drinking my first Grappa of this trip, as I write this chronicle.

Colette's Version

Didn't phone Tiziana as we decided to get moving. Went to Baptistry and Duomo and then on to Fidenza and then Pavia. Good day. David saw lots of little chaps in armour. We had super ice-cream (coffee flavour by Motte) and we spent about £5 on 1 lb (half kilo) of Parmesan. Cheaper (I think) lunch in a bar, three ham and cheese rolls, coke, mineral water and sweets (choc and fruit gums) for £2.50. Still more expensive it seems than England. Can't understand it; we're trying to be so careful. Very hot and humid; this is bothering me a lot. Also a certain pain in my pelvic area, which sometimes makes it very uncomfortable to walk. David cashed £100 in Parma. Stopped in small locanda on our way to Como (not far from Swiss border). Much cheaper (£8.60 per night). Just the sort of clean, homey place I've been after. Stopped at 5.30 or so. Nice to wash and rest up a bit before supper.

Tuesday 3rd July – Map: 19 Constance, Italy

David's Version

So far so much the better. Got clear across Switzerland without problems, though this lack of insurance (we had been unable to purchase travel insurance for western Europe) is really starting to worry me. Started the day at a good time and went straight into Como. Not too much trouble finding the church of Sant'Abbondio. The wall-paintings here were well worth the visit. Seem to show the most northerly version of the type of cuir-bouilli (*hardened leather used in armour*) seen so much in the south of Italy. Bought two rolls of film and some more petrol, which knocked chunks out of our finances. The drive across Switzerland was relatively easy, despite St. Bernard Pass, because the roads were so good. Found Zillis and its church with a painted ceiling. So far Switzerland, despite still being expensive, seems to give better value for money when it comes to road-side snacks than Italy. Reached Constance around 5 o'clock and decided to see the Cathedral before looking for accommodation. Hunted high and low for the carved warriors wearing poncho-type coats-of-plates. Eventually tracked them down on the inside of a <u>round</u> tomb *(actually the Mauritius Rundkapelle)*. More accessible than might have been expected. Had to dive back a few yards into Switzerland to change our francs into marks. Only a few miles further on found B & B for 45 DM for two. Next door had an excellent, and large, meal plus beer. Once again very good value for money.

Youth calls to youth while mum looks on a little nervously;
Freddie with a kitten at Como.

The wall-paintings in the Basilica of Sant'Abbondio in Como might not be the finest works of mid-14th century Italian art, but few others shed such light on the mixed armour and military equipment used in northern Italy at this time.

Colette's Version

Evening meal, room and breakfast came to £18. Finally we're doing something right. Headed for Switzerland, over St. Bernard Pass (freezing at top!) and into Germany at Lake Constance. Nice day, David's research went well, but I'm suffering from a bit of nausea and belching. Is it the sudden altitude rise? Made me feel unwell for a while, but a lovely meal of wienerschnitzel, chips and salad, and David's roast pork, beer, etc.(all at £10), made things feel right again. Better value and quantity for money than we've had for a long time. We find it more sensible to get a variety of food on our plates, which Freddie can share, rather than getting a small portion of rice or anything just for him. They charge far too much and also give too large a dish for him, which we end up eating anyway. Weather has turned cold. Freddie's cradle cap looks horrid. Wish I had brought cradocap shampoo, but at least I've covered his head with baby oil before going to bed. Forgot potty in car! This zimmer plus breakfast comes to £15. Don't think we could find anything cheaper.

Some dramatic scenery in south-eastern Switzerland, on the road from the Italian frontier to the village of Zillis, plus very green fields with very domesticated animals.

Zillis might be a small and little-known Swiss village,
but it has a beautifully located church dating from the 8th century.

The remarkable painted wooden ceiling in the Church of S. Martegn in Zillis in south-eastern Switzerland dates from 1130-40 AD.

Already helping daddy find "armoured chaps", Freddie stands proudly next to the carved Holy Sepulchre in the Mauritius Rundkapelle of Constance Cathedral. It took David some time - with a little assistance from the youngest available scholar - to track down these carvings.

The objects of their quest were mid-13th century Sleeping Guards in the Holy Sepulchre of the Mauritius Rundkapelle. The lower of the two not only wears an early form of cuirass but shows how it was laced or buckled at the back.

Wednesday 4th July – Map: 20 Ittenheim, near Strasbourg, France

David's Version

Once again a good and relatively easy day. Had to rush to the next village to change money to pay the B & B. Then easy drive through dismal weather and dark forests to Freiburg. Many more tourists here, many of them Americans. The Cathedral was splendid, though my carved figures were hard to see and difficult to photograph. Did, however, find some additional carvings. Centre of town a mixture of picturesque and tasteful modern, with the local tradition of crude-rude humour (a gargoyle on the Cathedral shitting into the street) being continued in a set of fountain statues projecting water from various orifices. Next stop Strasbourg. Went to Elizabeth's flat first (*David's cousin, who was living in Strasbourg with her husband at this time*). Fortunately she was in. Unfortunately her phone didn't work, but I got the Balesdent's (*in-laws of Colette's sister Suzanne, who were living outside the little town of Ittenheim, in Alsace near Strasbourg*) on a public call-box. So began a more relaxing few days. As it happened we'd turned up on Liz and John's wedding anniversary, so we really couldn't impose that evening. Had a splendid meal in a village restaurant just beyond Ittenheim, only slightly marred by Freddie falling off his chair and also leaking crap from his nappy during the hors d'oeuvre. Thence to Balesdents who made us very welcome indeed. Long chat and a late night.

It took Freddie some time to appreciate the delights of German sausages, even those fresh from a Grillwürste stall outside the Cathedral in Freiburg-im-Breisgau.

More to Freddie's taste was a rather naughty German fountain in the same city.

Colette's Version

Stopped at Freiburg. Nice Cathedral, market, sausage in a roll for lunch. Strasbourg. Went directly to Liz's flat in p.m. Phoned the Balesdent family (*Colette's sister's in-laws*) and they were waiting for us early evening. Had a good meal in a nearby village before getting there so they didn't have to worry about food. Freddie overexcited and didn't get to sleep until 10.30!

Almost as difficult to find as their cousins in Constance Cathedral were the carvings of Sleeping Guards at the Holy Sepulchre in the Cathedral of Freiburg im Breisgau in south-western Germany. These date from c.1330.

Cousin Elizabeth and her husband John, now lacking his once abundant beard, in Strasbourg where John was then working.

It was only when we got together in Strasbourg that Colette and Elizabeth realized that they were "due" at a very similar time.

Thursday 5th July – Map: 21 Ittenheim, near Strasbourg, France

David's Version

Spent most of the day sight-seeing in Strasbourg. In the morning "did" the Musée l'Oeuvre Notre Dame, but failed to get inside the Cathedral itself. Lunch with Elizabeth and back to the Balesdents' rather late. Incidentally, also got inside St. Guillaume's Church - unofficially - by finding a small open door and then exploring. Found a splendid painted wooden relief panel of a man being armed by his servants *(actually the man was a saint being martyred!)*. Late 15th century? *(actually early 16th century)*. Knew of it from Ffoulkes' book (C.J. Ffoulkes, *The Armourer and his Craft*, London 1912) but didn't realise it was here. Back to Balesdents', where Denya (Mrs. Balesdent) had almost finished translating the last two pages of my Trier talk *(later that summer David would present a paper entitled "Armes et Armures dans les Épopées de la Croisade" at the First International Colloquy on Les Épopées de la Croisade at Trier, 6-11 August 1984)*. Finished this after supper. Another late night after another pleasant day.

Colette's Version

Lie-in until 8. Musée near Cathedral at 10.30 and then lunch at Liz's. Pork-pie from M&S (*Marks & Spencer's high quality British grocery*), along with salad, rolls, and strawberries and yoghurt for dessert. Ice water with slices of lemon a good idea. Freddie had his nap as David visited another church and discovered he could not post Katherine's package. (*We had brought this from Jordan to be posted in Europe because our friend Katherine did not want to risk it being opened by Jordanian Export Customs officials – what on earth was in it?*)

Lurking out of sight of the casual visitor to the Church of St. William in Strasbourg - or to anyone not prepared to push at unlocked doors - is this superb carved and painted wooden panel portraying the martyrdom of a mail-clad saint. Dating from the very early 16th century, it clearly illustrates the armoured cod-piece beloved of some Hollywood film-makers.

Friday 6th July – Map: 22 Ittenheim, near Strasbourg, France

David's Version

Really played the tourist today. In the morning finally got rid of Katherine's box by sending it by rail to her parent's address. Next got ferry tickets across Channel (*to be prepared for our crossing in the near future*). Gone midday by time hit road south. Drove to Selestat where the church was shut, so no wall painting, but tasted some wine and bought a box of four bottles for dad. On the way back we followed the Route du Vin. Very picturesque, gentle country with the Vosges off to the left. Most of the small towns or villages seem to have had their medieval gates intact. Straight to Liz's flat again. Awaited John (who no longer has a beard) and then out for a Yugoslav meal in the same building on Rue des Veaux. Pretty good value. Had left car window open - I think wound down by Freddie. More care needed in future. Back for an even later night at the Balesdents'.

Colette's Version

Got ferry ticket. Posted Katherine's package at PP Station (£8!). Left at around noon to drive south. Lunch at Selestat, Freddie ate quiche. Bought "Vin d'Alsace" at Bergheim, two of Riesling and two of Guwerztraminer. Poodled along Route des Vins, and then to Yugoslav restaurant for supper with Liz and John. Rice too spicey with my meal, and others had goulash with potatoes which luckily Freddie would eat. Gave him a bad case of the shits the following day. Freddie had rolled David's window in car down and we only noticed it when we were ready to go home! Freddie getting to sleep even later than before (11 pm). How am I ever to get him into a routine?

With the Balesdent family in front of the magnolia tree in the garden of their home outside the little town of Ittenheim near Strasbourg.

Saturday 7th July – Map: 23 Ittenheim, near Strasbourg, France

David's Version

The quietest day of all. Up late, played in garden with Freddie, walked around Ittenheim and saw a TV crew filming a brass band in one of the posher farms. After lunch went into town (*Strasbourg*) with the Balesdents to see Caroline and from there to see Denya's mother and aunt. A fascinating old lady *(Denya's mother)* who lived in a splendid flat full of paintings. Her husband had been a leader of the Resistance in Strasbourg and had been numerously decorated for it. They were both involved in a "Lifeline" for Allied airmen and in helping young Alsatians avoiding service in the German Army from 1940 to 1945. Quite a story, part of which has been published and the rest of which is tied up with other documents in West Point in the USA until 1995. Kept her talking a bit too long, but it really was interesting *(See Appendix – Dr. Georges Sackenreiter's role in the Resistance)*. Back for a good supper, then talking, looking at books and old souvenirs. Freddie went to bed far too late and we all suffered for it.

Colette's Version

Morning of hand laundry and then walk around Ittenheim. Afternoon drive around city and then to pick up Caroline and to visit Denya's mother, a very interesting 84 year old whose husband was a leader of the Resistance during the war. Also met her sister, quiet and couldn't speak English. Again a mad rush to find a Pharmacie still open for nappies. Almost forgot that tomorrow is Sunday. Freddie is in a terrible routine. Supper too late (after 8 pm) and overexcitement as usual. I'm not getting him to bed until 10.30 and after that I'm shattered.

Freddie's fascination with running water was a theme than ran throughout this trip. Here his mother holds him securely at the village fountain in Selestat in Alsace.

Sunday 8th July – Map: 24 Arras, France

David's Version

A hard drive day. Got away very well and pressed on, mostly on Autoroutes - which are particularly pricey in France - stopping to look at Metz Cathedral, and aiming for St. Quentin or Cambrai. Couldn't find any accommodation until Arras. Here we seem to have struck lucky with price. Not too late and it should make tomorrow easy. I had Algerian couscous for supper, Colette having steak and chips. Being a long, sweaty day it was the beer that really counted, however.

Colette's Version

Said our goodbyes with Freddie screaming all the time to "go out". Motorway to Metz and Cathedral. Kept on motorway for a long way and must have covered 300 miles. Lunch in a bar/café (that's the way to keep prices down). Almost half a baguette each filled with saucisson, and Freddie had his fair share. Looked for about 1-1½ hours for a hotel, and finally found one in Arras for under £10. As usual, for supper I had to get something Freddie would eat - chips - with steak. David had couscous, which I would have had. This I find has been one of the difficulties – I sometimes long to taste different food, but because of Freddie, and because my stomach is a bit delicate, I have to be "conservative". Again Freddie asleep at 10.30 - how am I going to get him back to a good routine. Why is he like this?

1. We stop too late, and therefore…
2. We eat too late.
3. He gets overexcited.
4. He has slept quite a bit of the journey.

The Epitaph of Jacques Poulain, a benefactor of the Cathedral of Metz, with a painting of the Virgin Mary, dating from 1379 AD. At that time Metz was a city-republic within the Holy Roman Empire.

Monday 9th July – London, England

David's Version

Only noteworthy events were driving along rather than across the Western Front, the fact that Lille Cathedral apparently does <u>not</u> have an early 12th century font, a dismal crossing of the Channel in a boat delayed by 1½ hours, fish and chips on the A2, getting into Britain on Jordanian plates, and getting back to Linden Cottage (*David's father's house in Mill Hill, London*) without further disasters. I wonder what the journey back to Jordan will be like.

Colette's Version

(Just a date, nothing actually written for this, the day we finally got back to England. The exhaustion in the photo below says it all!)

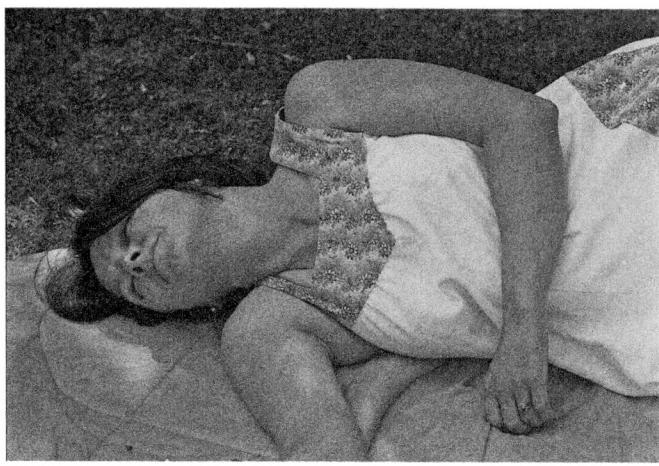

Colette sleeping on the grass on a lovely warm summer's day after we had finally got safely back to "England, home and beauty".

Aftermath

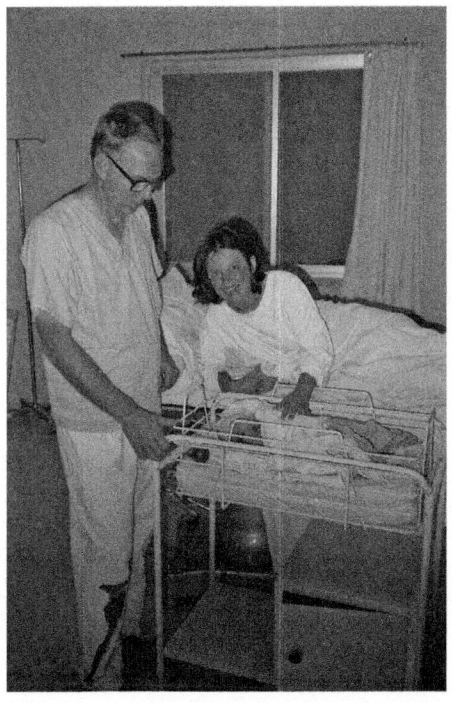

Colette, the doctor *(who was American and so fortunately spoke English)* and Antoinette within minutes of her birth.

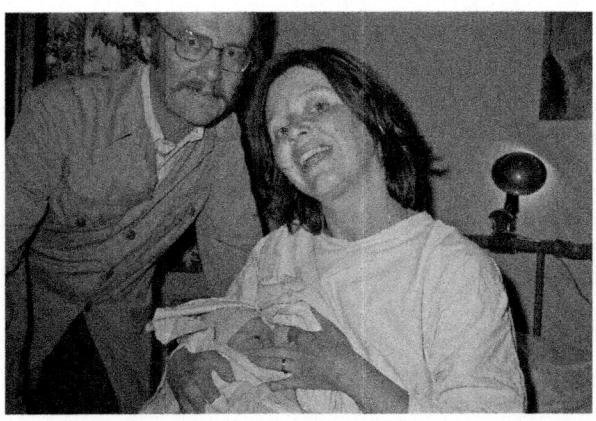

Proud mother, proud father, and Antoinette getting her first feed.

Freddie meets his sister for the first time at the Hospital.

Within a little over nine months from conception Colette gave birth to Antoinette, henceforth known as Nette for the classic reason that young Freddie could not get his tongue around his new sister's somewhat elaborate Christian name, our daughter Antoinette Laura Nicolle being named after her grandmothers. Colette's mother was Marie Antoinette Giroux, though always called Antoinette, and David's late mother being Laura Violet Nicolle. Having been created in a rather primitive Jordanian government resthouse-hotel next to the famous Crusader castle of Kerak in southern Jordan, Antoinette was born in the Baptist Missionary Hospital at Anjara, overlooking another historic castle, the splendid Saracen fortress at Ajlun on 17th October 1984. That same day there was a minor earthquake. Having thus been credited with "making the earth to move" twice, firstly at Kerak and secondly at Ajlun, the newly emergent Antoinette had also already managed to travel several thousands of miles under far from easy conditions. Sadly she was unaware of the epic journey that she had taken, being in her mother's womb at the time. The as-yet unborn and unnamed Antoinette was similarly unaware that her mother Colette had returned to Jordan in the more comfortable circumstances with Royal Jordanian Airlines. Not surprisingly, her doctor in England strongly advised against repeating the journey overland. Instead David drove alone after attending the first days of the Colloquy at Trier (see above). It took him eighteen days but he was rewarded by an enthusiastic welcome on reaching Yarmouk University. According to his final diary entry of 23 August 1984; "....straight as an arrow to Southern Housing where the rest of the day was spent in joyful reunions and a lot of unpacking. Freddie freaked!!"

Ajlun Castle on the evening of the day after Antoinette's birth, seen from Colette's room in the Baptist Missionary Hospital at Anjara.

A cut-away reconstruction of Ajlun Castle, painted by Stuart Priest in 1995 to illustrate an article by David (Saracen Strongholds: Saracen castles during the Crusades, <u>Military Illustrated</u>, vol. 83, April 1995).

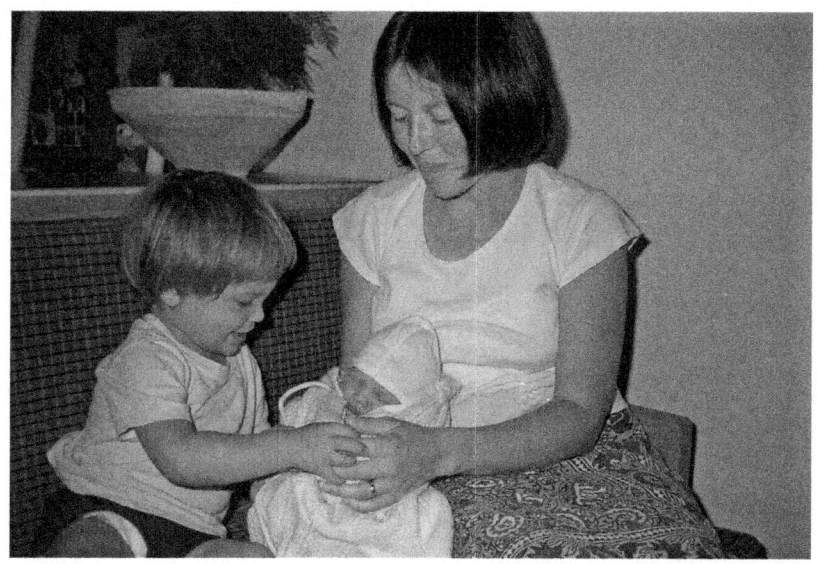

Back in our flat in Southern Housing, the relationship between brother and sister started well, and has continued as such ever since.

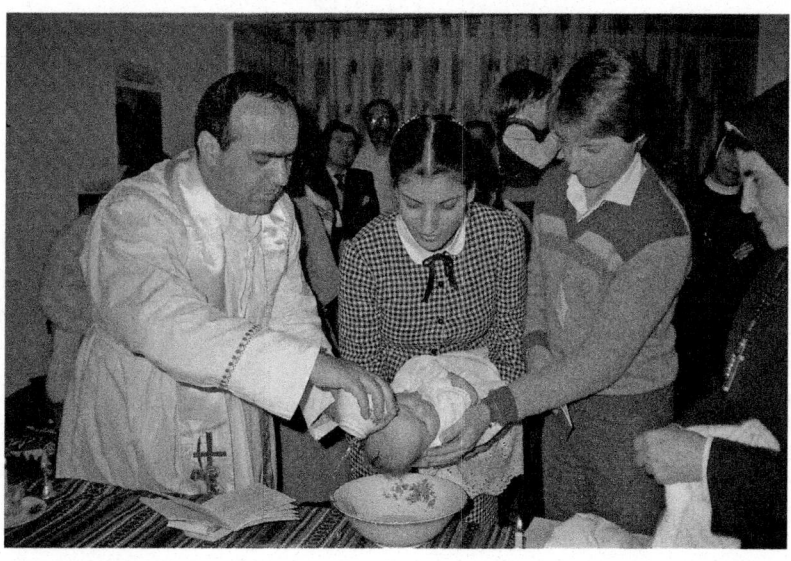

Antoinette's Christening, with Father Farah pouring the water while Suheila and Peter Lewis stand in as surrogate god-parents for Colette's sister and brother, Michele and Rich, who were unable to come from the United States to Jordan for the ceremony.

Antoinette spent the first two and three-quarter years of her life enjoying the sort of unfettered childhood which few save ex-pats in a so-called third world country can enjoy. As one might expect, she can now recall nothing of this except the haziest of images and impressions.

Antoinette already the bell of the ball, with Arts Faculty students at the Yarmouk University Festival early in 1985.

Brother and sister together on a swing in the playground of Eastern Housing where we moved to get more room in 1985. This was shortly after King Hussain's birthday, hence the banner.

Ever the glutton for punishment . . .

David made a second attempt to see and photograph some of the painted monastic churches of Moldavia in late summer 1985. This time he returned from London to Irbid via northern Romania in a new white Fiat Panda, having sold the earlier black Panda. Colette had wisely decided to take the children, Freddie now coming up to three years old and Antoinette coming up to one year, back to Jordan by air.

David had also purchased a small trailer in which to transport some useful but quite substantial baby-related items. Sadly, this trailer was "nicked" outside a hotel in Bulgaria, chosen because a hotel seemed to be more secure than a camp-site, especially as it was across the street from the local police station. As a consequence, Freddie and Antoinette had to spend their first years without some of the things which they have more recently acquired for their own offspring. All David gained, apart from some splendid photographs of Moldavian art and architecture, was a tow-hook which was never again used.

Our second Fiat Panda - the white one - in the Carpathian Mountains of northern Moldavia between Moldoviţa and Sucevita, during another drive from London to Irbid in the late summer of 1985. Then a notably wild part of the country where bears roamed, it is now a centre for winter sports and summer hiking known as Suceviţa Ciumârna or Tiroliana Palma.

Part of a wall-painting on the exterior of the Church at Moldoviţa Monastery in Moldavia, dating from 1532-37 AD. As part of an illustration of the Fall of Constantinople to the Ottoman Turks in 1453, it might symbolize the Orthodox Christian Principality of Moldavia's continuing struggle against the Muslim Turks.

Postscript

Not until the summer of 2007 was a doting father in a position to fulfil his longstanding promise to take Antoinette back to Jordan, to the now greatly expanded town of Irbid, and the now rather more impressive Yarmouk University Campus. With her brother, now graduated from Freddie to Fred, her mother and her father, Antoinette visited several of the other remarkable sites and sights of Jordan. Furthermore, having initially flown into Syria, there was the added bonus of nearly a week in the astonishing medieval city of Damascus before heading for Jordan. There we hired a car and had several adventures, though nothing quite on the scale of the summer of '84.

Colette had hardly changed at all by 2007 when David was able to fulfil a long-standing promise to take his children back to where they had spent some of their earliest years. We flew first into Damascus, to sample the old city's superb freshly pressed orange juice.

Over the years we built up something of a special relationship with "Sultan", a shop in the famous covered Suq Hamidiyah in Damascus. So it was natural that we went there to buy some souvenirs, though not the turbans and veils worn here by Colette and Antoinette.

Back to Yarmouk University for the first time since 1987, meeting the new Head of the Faculty of Arts, Prof. Mahmoud Sadiq.

Fred in the infants' class at Yarmouk Model School, to be followed by St. Mary's Primary School, Loughborough Grammar School, and University of Cambridge. Antoinette, never reaching school age in Jordan, followed Fred to St. Mary's, then Our Lady's Convent School in Loughborough, University of Oxford, and a PhD from University College London.

Antoinette outside the hospital where she was born, with Ajlun castle still dominating the skyline.

Fred perhaps following in his father's tyre-tracks, driving our hire-car through some dramatic scenery in southern Jordan.

Brother and sister still getting on well, this time on the veranda of the restaurant at Umm Qays.[14] The columns are still here but fortunately the Jordan Army trenches have largely disappeared.

Colette still patiently listening to her husband droning on about something archaeological, and David still lugging about his excessively large camera-case. That at least would soon be relegated to storage.

Appendix – Dr. Georges Sackenreiter's role in the Resistance

Following our visit to Strasbourg when we met the grandmother of Colette's brother-in-law Georges-Eric, Colette and David asked Georges-Eric for more detail about his impressive maternal grandparents. This is their story:

Georges Sackenreiter was a well-known surgeon and a director of surgical clinics in Strasbourg and Saverne (or *Zàwere* in Alsatian German, a town and commune 45 km north-west of Strasbourg). He was married to Marie-Thérèse Sackenreiter (née Zeyssolff).

Dr. Georges and Marie-Thérèse Sackenreiter
(from Georges-Eric Balesdent family archive).

During the Second World War, with the German annexation of Alsace and neighbouring Lorraine (1940-44), approximately 130,000 young men from Alsace and Lorraine were forcibly conscripted into the German armed forces. These were known as the *malgré-nous* or "despite us". Dr. Sackenreiter used his medical expertise and reputation to help young Alsatian men avoid or delay such conscription by writing falsified or exaggerated medical reports concerning their supposed injuries or diseases. This he also did for men threatened with forced conscription into German labour corps, such as the *Reichsartbeitsdienst*, because Alsace was now classed as part of the German Reich rather than occupied French territory. This only proved possible because Georges Sackenreiter was part of a tight-knit community of doctors, pharmacists and other health workers. In fact, between autumn 1942 and the day of liberation, the records of the hospital in which he worked show that hundreds of people had been helped in this way.

Dr. Sackenreiter also made contact with at least one Resistance network and through them he and his family were able to help downed Allied airmen, escaped prisoners and displaced or persecuted persons including entire families. On one occasion there were no less than three such *flüchtlinge* families in the Sackenreiter's summer house at Thannenkirch in the Vosges mountains.

This was highly dangerous work and the Sackenreiter family, along with the rest of the French population, were hugely relieved when Strasbourg was liberated by the Free French 2nd Armoured Division and First French Army on 23rd November 1944. However, on the last day of 1944 the German Army launched its last major counter-offensive on the Western Front (*Operation Nordwind* - 31st December 1944 to 25th January 1945) which, though it did not get very far, caused Allied forces to pull back from part of northern Alsace. General Alexander McCarrel Patch, the Commander of the US 7th Army, was actually a guest of the Sackenreiter family at the time. He is thought to have warned the doctor and his family to flee their home in Saverne because Georges Sackenreiter's name had been seen on a document in the local Gestapo office, listing those due to be executed. The warning might, however, have come from a British intelligence source, through their agent in the area, Dr. Sarafian.

Lt. Gen. Patch (right) and Lt. Gen. Devers in France in January 1945
(public domain photo).

After the war Dr. Sackenreiter received the Médaille de la Résistance *"for helping and assisting escaped prisoners* (of war) *and refractories* (including members of the Resistance who were on the run). *Also for assisting and providing* (civilian) *clothing for downed Allied airmen"*. The question of clothing was more difficult than might be thought. During the war, and under German rule, clothing and textiles became increasingly scarce. Eventually there were no spare clothes to give to Allied escapees, so clothing had to be returned once an escapee had reached safety. One member of the organisation later recalled that he had a suit *"which had been to Marseilles nine times and had returned to us nine times"*.

Endnotes

[1] **Palmyra** – The ruins of the Roman and pre-Islamic Arab city of Palmyra in the Syrian Desert.

[2] **Meskene** – The site of the medieval Islamic town of Meskene on the river Euphrates was flooded as a result of the building of the Tabka Dam and the formation of Lake Assad; however,. archaeologists transferred its famous minaret to the edge of the escarpment overlooking the new lake.

[3] **Jerash** – The ruins of the largely Roman and early Byzantine city of Jerash are one of the marvels of the Kingdom of Jordan. Since 1981 the annual Jerash Festival for Culture and Arts has also been held here.

[4] **Deir ez-Zor** – The main city on the River Euphrates in eastern Syria.

[5] **Raqqa** – A small city on the Euphrates river in north-central Syria, famous for its early medieval Islamic architecture and more

recently for being the de facto capital of the so-called Islamic State of Iraq and the Levant from 2013 until 2017.

[6] **Baghdad Gate** – The most famous architectural survival from the early medieval Islamic period in Raqqa is the Baghdad Gate, named because the road to Baghdad exited Raqqa through this gate. It is believed to date from the 8th century.

[7] **Qalaat Jaber** – A huge brick fortress on a narrow escarpment overlooking the north bank of the River Euphrates several kilometres upriver from Raqqa. Since the construction of the Tabka Dam, the ruins of the fortress of Qalaat Jaber overlook Lake Assad at one of its broadest points.

[8] **Abu Hurayrah** – The virtually abandoned site of Abu Hurayrah in the Euphrates Valley east of Aleppo was one of the most important locations to be excavated by archaeologists before the filling of Lake Assad. It was inhabited from Neolithic times until the Middle Ages, though with several periods of abandonment in between. The medieval minaret does not appear to have been saved.

[9] **Delfin** – The Aero L-29 Delfin was a jet trainer, built in Czechoslovakia and used throughout much the Soviet bloc, as well as being exported to several Arab countries including the Syrian Air Force, where these aeroplanes retained a "silver" or bare metal finish.

[10] **Deir Semaan** – The ruined early Byzantine monastery of Deir Semaan, with its Church of Saint Simeon Stylites, is perhaps the most famous of what are known as the Dead Cities of northern Syria.

[11] **Bagras castle** – The forbidding black stone castle of Bagras is built upon a steep hill in what is now the Hatay province of Turkey, not far from Antakya (Antioch). Part of what can be seen today dates from the 12th-13th century Crusader period.

[12] **Göreme, Cappadocia** – The rock-cut Byzantine and post-Byzantine painted churches of Cappadocia in central Turkey lie within the Göreme National Park, which became a UNESCO World Heritage Site in 1985, the year after we visited the area during our overland drive from Jordan to England.

[13] **Bayazit Mosque** – There are number of mosques dating from the Ottoman period which are credited to Sultan Bayazit (1389-1402 AD). The one in Bolu was replaced by a new Grand Mosque, built in 1899 - a fact not made clear in my guide book!

[14] **Umm Qays** – The beautifully located Roman ruins of Umm Qays, the biblical Gadara, overlook both the Jordan and Yarmouk Valleys as well as the Sea of Galilee. Colette and David used to take the children there for picnics when they lived in Jordan.

Printed in Great Britain
by Amazon